IN YOUR LANE

Harness Your Inner Talents,
Ignite Your Passion, and Craft a
Purpose-Driven Life

KELVIN OSONDU

ISBN: 9798862338195

Edited and Published by KayVee Books

To all seekers of purpose and personal growth: May your journey be filled with clarity, courage, and countless inspiring moments.

CONTENTS

INTRODUCTION

I have often pondered what sets some folks on a path that seems to shine a little brighter. And I'm not just talking about having fancy cars or big houses. I'm talking about that deep-down, heartwarming feeling of contentment that comes from making a real difference in the world.

You know, I've spent a good chunk of my life diving into the idea of finding your own way in this world. But let me tell you, it's been a bit of a rocky road, especially when it comes to writing this book. I had to be patient and grow in ways I never expected just to be able to share this message about discovering your own unique path.

So, if you're curious about how you can find your own lane in life, stick around. We're about to embark on a journey together, like two friends exploring a new trail. I've got stories to tell, lessons to share, and a warm cup of wisdom to pour out. Together, we'll uncover the secrets to that special kind of success that fills your heart with joy.

But before we dive in, let me give you a little taste of what's to come. This book isn't about chasing after riches or fame. No, it's about finding that sweet spot where you feel like you're exactly where you're meant to be. It's about discovering your unique talents and passions, and then using them to make the world a better place. You see, success isn't just about what you can get; it's also about what you can give.

Now, let me share a little secret with you. I believe that each one of us has a purpose in this grand tapestry of life. Yep, that includes you, my friend. You have something special inside you, a talent or a calling that's uniquely yours. And when you find it, when you really embrace it, amazing things can happen.

But I get it; it's not always easy to figure out what that something special is. That's where our journey begins. Over the pages of this book, we'll explore the twists and turns of my own path, and how I found my lane. I'll share the lessons I've learnt along the way, the moments of inspiration that lit up my journey, and the challenges that made me stronger.

You see, I didn't wake up one day with all the answers. Nope, it took time, patience, and a fair share of stumbles. But those stumbles, my friend, they were all part of the adventure. They taught me things I couldn't have learnt any other way. And I'm here to pass those lessons on to you.

So, whether you're just starting to wonder about your own path or you've been searching for a while, know that you're in good company. We're going to dig deep, we're going to ask some big questions, and we're going to discover the incredible power of finding your own lane in life.

Get ready for an adventure. We're about to set off on a journey that could change your life forever.

PART I

PURPOSE

INTRODUCTION TO PURPOSE

Think of purpose like the threads that make a big warm blanket. It's what makes us feel important and gives our life meaning. It's also like a bright light that shows us the way in life. Finding our purpose is something we all do. It's like taking a trip where we learn about ourselves, discover unexpected things, and suddenly everything makes more sense.

Let me tell you about John C. Maxwell. His story is a great example of how someone can find their purpose by not giving up, getting better, and listening to what they're meant to do.

Dr Maxwell started as a church pastor. He spent years working in the church, helping and guiding people. He was really good at it and did it with a lot of dedication. He shared his wisdom and comforted those who needed it.

But deep down, Dr Maxwell felt like there was something more he should be doing. While being a pastor satisfied part of his desire to help, he had other talents he hadn't explored yet. He didn't know that the next part of his life would show him what his real purpose was.

One day, while teaching a group of 31 pastors, something unexpected happened. The pastors loved his teaching so much that they wanted more. They told him to keep sharing his insights. This made Dr Maxwell realise something important. He wasn't just meant to be a pastor; he was also meant to be a coach, a trainer, and a helper of leaders.

This realisation was a big deal. Dr Maxwell discovered that his purpose was even bigger than he thought. The joy he felt while guiding and training others was incredible. He realised that his true calling was to motivate and empower people, making the world a better place. This clear understanding pushed him to leave his role as a pastor and start a new journey in coaching and training. This decision allowed him to reach millions of people around the world, not just one group.

With his new purpose, Dr Maxwell began a mission to help leaders and create positive change on a large scale. He became an author, writing more than 80 books read by millions worldwide. His words crossed borders and languages, touching people's hearts and inspiring them to become better leaders. John C. Maxwell's journey shows how finding and following your purpose can change your life and the lives of many others.

Now, let me share my story. When I was young, I really liked writing stories. I'd use words to create these magical tales that felt like they came alive on the pages of my notebooks. But I didn't know that this love for writing would connect with my search to find my special reason for being here. It's like these two things, my love for stories and finding my purpose, came together to shape where I'm going in life.

During those early years, I was curious about something else too—the world of computers. I was fascinated by technology, so I decided to study computer science. I wanted to be like Mark Zuckerberg, creating digital empires with innovation and code. But the more I learnt about software, the further I felt from the passion that had driven me.

Yet, I couldn't ignore my love for writing. Since I was 16, I'd been typing away on keyboards, crafting pages filled with fantasy stories. I loved these tales, but I hadn't yet connected this talent to a bigger purpose. These stories were like secret signs of my purpose, hidden behind the demands of another journey.

Change came in an unexpected way when I joined a group coaching programme. In the pages of a self-help book, a new understanding unfolded—a realisation that would untangle the connections between my passion, skills, and purpose. As I read the book, a spark lit up inside me, giving me a deep appreciation for personal growth and self-improvement.

With each page of self-help books, I felt myself changing and growing. The words from authors who had walked their own paths of growth spoke to me. Through these books, I came to understand that my deep desire to help others was part of my purpose. The wish to lift people up, motivate them, and show them the way had been with me on my journey, but now I saw its real importance.

This realisation was life-changing. I saw that my writing skills, my fascination with technology, and my urge to help others were all connected by the thread of purpose.

Writing wasn't just a hobby anymore; it was a way to share knowledge, spark inspiration, and bring about positive change. My interest in computers wasn't leading me astray; it was a path to use my talents for a greater good.

This newfound clarity helped me see the difference between my skills and my purpose. I embraced writing as a way to touch lives, make people think, and create positive change. My journey wasn't just about computer code; it was about writing stories that empowered and enriched lives. This realisation brought me an incredible sense of fulfilment, like the last pieces of a puzzle falling into place.

As I look back on my journey, I see the moments of chance that led me here. My early love for writing, my curiosity about technology, and my strong desire to help others were all part of a grand plan, a mix of talents and passions guiding me toward my purpose. Discovering your purpose is like a journey with experiences, choices, and moments when everything suddenly makes sense. It's a journey that needs patience, self-reflection, and the readiness to follow your heart's whispers.

Sadly, not everyone finds their purpose in

life. It's like finding a hidden treasure. And once you discover it, the desire to fulfil that purpose never stops. Some people have been taught to ignore their purpose. They go to school, get a job, get married, have kids and grandkids, and one day, they're gone. Imagine being a spoon in a kitchen, sitting in a drawer, never getting to do what you were meant for, until one day, the owner moves away and tosses you in the trash. It's a bit sad, right? Well, that's how some people live – without excitement or a real reason. My wish is that if you're reading this and haven't found your purpose yet, you start looking for it. Because life doesn't make much sense if you don't know why you're here and what you're meant to do.

What is Purpose?

Let's pause for a moment and talk about what purpose really means. According to the Cambridge Dictionary, purpose is "why you do something and why something exists." When someone feels they don't have purpose, it's like they're saying they don't know why they're here. Dr. Myles Monroe, in his book 'Pursuit of Purpose,' talked about this. He said, "If you don't have a purpose, time doesn't mean much, energy doesn't have a reason, and life feels uncertain."

Here's the deal: everything in life, including you, has a reason for being here. Purpose is the reason (why) behind your life. Even before you were born, there was a reason for you. Think of a car. The person who made the car had a reason (purpose) for making it. But until the car is used for that reason, it's just an object. You don't buy a car and then never drive it, right? You drive it to do what it was made for. It's the same with you. You need to actively figure out your purpose and do things that match it to live a fulfilling life.

I believe there are two main types of purpose that everyone should discover and live by. Some folks focus on one and forget about the other. But it's essential to understand both types of purpose.

Collective Purpose

We all share a common purpose. This type of purpose helps us live peacefully and get along with others. It's one of the big reasons we're here. You don't need to spend ages figuring out this kind of purpose. It's quite straightforward. Our collective purpose is to love and assist one another. It doesn't make much sense to learn new skills or gather tons of knowledge if you don't know how to care for and support others.

In my last book about Identity, I stressed the importance of helping others. I genuinely believe that humans are meant to lend a hand to each other. If you only think about yourself, it can create a lot of issues. Sometimes, the real reason some folks feel down is because they're not helping others. They're solely focused on themselves. If you take a closer look, no job is only about benefiting yourself. Whether you're a waiter in a restaurant or a lawyer in a courtroom, everyone does something to aid others. Even a mum at home is helping others by raising kids who will contribute positively to the community.

Individual Purpose

Now, let's dive into this kind of purpose, which often comes up when folks talk about chasing their life goals. Your individual purpose is all about using your talents to assist others. Unlike our collective purpose where everyone should lend a hand to one another, uncovering your individual purpose takes some self-discovery. In simple terms, you need to figure out what you're good at and what kind of person you are. It's a journey you lead, even though your family can support you along the way. But why family, you might ask? Well, I firmly believe that your parents play a big role in helping you discover what you're meant to do or who you're meant to be. They should be the first to spot the hidden talents within you. They might not know your personal purpose precisely, but they can steer you towards finding it. However, it's vital not to do something solely because your parents want you to. In the long run, you should also find joy in that pursuit.

Your individual purpose should always align with our collective purpose that we all share. It's like a puzzle piece that fits perfectly into the bigger picture. Using your talents should never harm others; it's about making things better for everyone. Your talents are like treasures meant to bring goodness and make our shared purpose a reality. Picture it like this:

imagine you have a unique gift that can make people smile or feel better. It wouldn't make sense to use that gift in a way that makes someone sad or hurts them. Your gift is there to spread happiness and contribute to the greater good. Just like how each star in the sky adds to the beauty of the night, your individual purpose should enhance the greater good we're all working towards.

BENEFITS OF PURPOSE

Once upon a time, in a bustling forest, there lived two furry friends: Sammy the Squirrel and Benny the Bunny. Sammy was known for his incredible speed, darting from tree to tree, gathering nuts with lightning-fast agility. Benny, on the other hand, possessed the gift of listening; he could hear the faintest rustle of leaves and knew the storeys of every creature in the forest.

One sunny morning, the two friends sat by a sparkling stream, sipping on sweet acorn tea. Sammy, with his paws still trembling from his morning nut chase, looked at Benny with envy.

"Ben," Sammy sighed, "I wish I had your special skills. You just sit there, listening, and it seems so easy."

Benny twitched his long ears and smiled. "Well, Sammy, I admire your speed and agility. But don't you see? We each have our unique talents. You dash around, collecting nuts that keep us fed through winter. My listening helps me understand our friends in the forest, and sometimes, I can help them when they're in need."

Sammy scratched his head, considering Benny's words. "So, you mean, we both have a purpose, right?"

"Exactly!" Benny nodded. "Our forest thrives because of what we each bring to it. Without your nuts, we'd go hungry. Without my listening, we might not know when someone needs a hand, or a paw, or a listening ear."

From that day on, Sammy and Benny embraced their special gifts. Sammy never wished for Benny's ears again, and Benny never envied Sammy's speed. They realised that their unique talents, when combined, made their forest a better place.

And so, the forest flourished, thanks to the realisation that every creature had its purpose. Sammy the Squirrel and Benny the Bunny became a reminder that our differences, when celebrated, enrich the tapestry of life.

In this chapter, I'll take a moment to share with you some benefits of discovering and pursuing your purpose. These benefits make life truly meaningful. I truly believe purpose isn't just a nice-to-have tool that you might consider having at some point in your life. I believe that as long as you're breathing, you have a purpose to fulfil. Let's begin.

Purpose Provokes Courage

Chasing your dreams is tough. It's like going on an adventure, and adventures need courage. Purpose gives you that courage. It's like a tool that helps you take brave steps, believing you'll succeed in the end. Sammy the Squirrel's journey in our story shows how finding your special role can make you brave.

At first, Sammy feels jealous of Benny the Bunny. He thinks Benny's listening skills are great, and he's worried that his fast nut-gathering isn't important. But as Sammy learns how crucial his job is in their forest, he gets the courage to face challenges. Sammy becomes brave when he realises his unique skills help the forest and its creatures. Benny also becomes courageous because he knows his listening and helping skills are valuable to others. Both of them find the strength to deal with tough times and protect their forest home.

Life can be comfy in your usual routine when you don't have a purpose. There's no big reason to do things differently. But when you have a purpose, it's like a built-in courage booster. It helps you make those tough, life-changing choices.

When I decided to leave Nigeria as a teenager, it was a scary decision. I wasn't going with my family; I was going all by myself. Back then, I didn't fully know my true purpose, but I did know what I needed for it: education. That's why I was able to go ahead with my plan to study in the United Kingdom. I think I could only do that because I had a sense of purpose. It gave me a strong reason to leave my comfort zone.

My parents also backed me up on this journey because they believed in the power of purpose. My mom always felt that I had a reason for being here, and that gave her the courage to let her teenage son go to another country.

Purpose Builds Confidence

To make tough choices that lead to success, you need courage. But it's also important to be confident in those choices. Sammy the Squirrel and Benny the Bunny's story shows how finding your unique purpose can give you that confidence boost.

At first, Sammy was jealous of Benny's great listening skills. But he later figured out that he also had an important role in their forest community with his speed and nut-gathering talents. Realising this made Sammy more confident. Benny, on the other hand, felt confident because he knew that his gift for listening and helping others really helped their forest friends. They both understood that their unique abilities had a purpose in their community.

Dr. Myles Munroe's book, "The Pursuit of Purpose," says, "Confidence helps us know if what we're doing is the right thing." When people tried to talk my parents out of letting me go to the UK, they stayed confident in their decision. Their purpose was clear: to give me the best education they could. This purpose gave them the confidence to make a tough choice. So, having a main purpose in life gives you the confidence that you have a reason for being here. You wake up each day feeling ready to offer something or help someone. This confidence makes it easier to learn new things and grow.

Purpose Empowers Perseverance

At the beginning, Sammy felt really down. He didn't believe in himself as a squirrel and envied Benny, who was a skilled bunny. But things changed when they both realised how important they were in their forest community. This made them understand their purpose.

Sammy had to gather nuts, which was super important for everyone to survive the winter. This purpose made him keep trying even when he doubted himself at first. Benny, on the other hand, was a great listener and helper. He felt more determined to help others when he realised how vital his role was.

Having a clear purpose can help you keep going, especially when things get tough. When I first came to the UK as an international student, finding a part-time job was really hard. I applied for lots of jobs, but they kept saying no because I didn't have UK work experience. I could have given up since my parents couldn't afford everything. But I had a purpose: I wanted to ease their burden and support myself. So, I didn't give up. I saw that having a job was part of fulfilling my purpose at the university. It was tough, but my purpose kept me going until the end.

Ever wondered why some people give up on their goals so easily? They can't seem to keep a job for long, and they always have a bunch of reasons for quitting. But the real reason is that they haven't found their purpose in life. When someone knows their purpose, they can stick with a job even if they don't like it because it's like a stepping stone to what they really want to do.

Think about Nelson Mandela. He spent 27 years in prison fighting against apartheid, a system of racial segregation in South Africa. But he had a strong purpose: to end apartheid and make his country fair for everyone. That purpose kept him going even in the toughest times. And because of his purpose, he's famous around the world, and he even won the Nobel Peace Prize for his leadership and good character.

Purpose Removes Distractions

When you have a purpose in your life, it's

easier to know what to say "no" to. Without a purpose, you might get caught up in all sorts of things because you don't have a good reason for being here. Purpose helps you avoid things that can distract you. Anything or anyone that takes you away from your purpose can be a problem for your future. But if you don't have a purpose, it's hard to see what might harm your future.

In the story about Sammy and Benny, they both get distracted at first. Sammy wants to hop like Benny, and Benny wants to gather nuts like Sammy. But as they discover their special roles in the forest, their purposes become clear. Sammy's purpose is to gather nuts, so he focuses on that and stops being distracted. Benny's purpose is to listen and help, so he concentrates on helping others. Having a purpose helps them avoid distractions and stay on track.

Over the years, I've learnt that people often get distracted when they don't have a clear purpose. This is especially common among millennials. You might be scrolling through social media and suddenly find yourself signing up for a 30-day weight loss programme or a way to make extra money online. But when you have a purpose, you're less likely to get sidetracked. You think about whether these new things fit with what you're really trying to do in life.

Once you know your purpose, it's easier to say "no" to things or people that don't help you. Not everyone who comes into your life is a good friend. Some people might actually get in the way of what you're trying to achieve, but if you haven't discovered your purpose, you might be easily influenced by what others want you to do. For example, if you need to study for an important test or presentation, you wouldn't waste your time talking about the latest TV show. It's okay to relax, but even fun activities can turn into distractions if you haven't figured out what you're really here to do.

Purpose Strengthens Your Vision

Dr. Myles Munroe's idea about vision is pretty cool. He says it's like being able to see the end of a journey right from the start. This is a bit like what Dr. Stephen Covey talks about in his book "The 7 Habits of Highly Effective People." Covey says that thinking about where you want to end up, or your "end," is something special that humans can do. But, here's the thing: having a clear vision of where you want to go is not enough. You need to have a strong "why" or reason for getting there. Without a good reason, you might never reach your goal. Some people might even get to their destination and not know what to do next because they didn't have a strong "why" pushing them in the first place.

At first, Sammy and Benny had different ideas about what they wanted to be — Sammy wanted to hop like Benny, and Benny wanted to gather nuts like Sammy. These mixed-up visions made things confusing and didn't work too well.

But when they figured out their special jobs — Sammy as a nut gatherer and Benny as a listener and helper — their visions became much clearer. Sammy knew he had to gather nuts quickly to help his forest friends. Benny knew he needed to listen and help others.

So, when you're thinking about what you want to be or do, it's important to ask yourself why. Why do you want to be a great lawyer, a famous actor, or anything else? Without a strong "why," even if you reach your goal, you might not feel as happy as you thought you would. Your "why" is like the fuel that keeps your vision going.

PRINCIPLES OF PURPOSE

Let's talk about some important things you need to know when it comes to finding your purpose in life. These are like guideposts to help you understand and discover your purpose. If you ignore these, it might make it harder to find your purpose. These are like the building blocks for living a purpose-filled life.

1. Everyone Has a Purpose

In a world with 8 billion people, it might seem like having a purpose is something only a few lucky ones get. But that's not true. Every one of us is born with a purpose. Just like the person who made the camera had a reason for making it, you have a reason for being here on Earth. Some people find this hard to believe because of their circumstances when they were born or how they grew up. But if you want to make a difference in the world, you first need to believe that you have a reason for being here.

Nobody else has lived the exact life you have. That's proof that you have a unique purpose during your time on Earth. Maybe you've faced tough times and felt like you couldn't do great things, and that made you think you don't matter. Well, I'm here to tell you that you do matter, and deep inside you, there's untapped potential and a purpose waiting to be discovered. Just because you haven't found your purpose yet doesn't mean it's not there. Sometimes, you just need to figure out how to find it.

You might wonder if you have a unique purpose if you're following in your parents' footsteps, like taking over the family business or having the same job they had. Well, let me tell you, that's perfectly fine. Sometimes, people are born with the purpose of carrying on a family tradition, and there's nothing wrong with that. Take Dwayne Johnson, also known as "The Rock," for example. He's a famous wrestler, and his dad was a wrestler too. But that didn't mean he didn't have his own purpose. He continued his dad's legacy and achieved even more. Before becoming a wrestler, he tried other things like playing

Canadian football and doing comedy. So, even though their careers seemed similar, Dwayne Johnson and his dad had different impacts on their generation. In other words, they had their own individual purposes.

You might feel like you don't have a purpose, especially if you come from a big family, and your parents praised your siblings more. But don't let that stop you from figuring out why you're here on Earth. As long as you're alive, you have a purpose to fulfil. After reading this book, make a decision not to give up until you find your purpose. Remember, our main human purpose is to help each other with love. You just need to figure out how to use your unique talents and experiences to help others.

2. Purpose is not the same as responsibility

Sometimes, it's not easy to tell the difference between your purpose and your responsibilities. But I want to make something clear: you can do one without the other. You can be a great dad without necessarily fulfilling your purpose. You could be an excellent teacher and not a perfect mom. Both parts of your life are important, but don't let one take over the other. Some people get so focused on achieving their purpose that they're willing to give up their family for it. On the flip side, some concentrate so much on creating a perfect home that they forget about their purpose in life.

Life can be tough, and sometimes you might have to put your purpose on hold to meet your responsibilities. This could mean taking a job that pays well to provide for your family or moving to a smaller town to raise your kids, even if it means giving up career opportunities in a big city. But it's not smart to ignore your responsibilities just to focus on your purpose. And the same goes for focusing solely on responsibilities while forgetting about your purpose.

There might be times when you have to prioritise one over the other. For example, a mom might decide to temporarily leave her career to take care of her kids because she sees it as her responsibility. But the problem can arise if she loses sight of her purpose in the process. When her kids are grown, she might feel lost and sad because she replaced her purpose with her responsibility.

In the subsequent chapters, I'll talk about dreams and how they relate to your purpose. When you have responsibilities that make you put your purpose on hold, it's crucial to keep your dream alive until you can fulfil your responsibilities. For instance, if you're in a job that doesn't fulfil you but provides for your family, hold on to your dream until you have the time and resources to follow your purpose. This might mean taking exams or courses to get the right job while working in one you don't love. Or it could mean saving money to start a business that will help you fulfil your purpose.

3. It Takes Courage to Live with Purpose

Life doesn't come with guarantees. Just because you're born into wealth doesn't mean you'll stay rich. Graduating from a top college doesn't promise you a job at a big company. There's no seat with your name on it waiting for you; that's just a myth. You need courage to figure out and do what you're meant to in life. This is where many people struggle. We're here to help and love each other, but often, people avoid doing what they should because they're scared of the work.

In my last year of high school, I was lucky to be on the basketball team. I practised with my friends, but when it was time for a real game, I hesitated to get on the court. Even though I dreamt of being an NBA player, I was too scared to play in my school's tournament. Maybe you've felt like this too? Yes, practise and having the right mindset can boost your confidence to help others. But without the courage to make a difference, it's hard to fulfil your purpose.

Think about it: your dreams and goals should be bigger than who you are now. You need courage to get closer to them.

4. Don't Neglect Your Individual Purpose

Life doesn't have much meaning without a purpose. We can all help each other, which is our shared purpose, but sometimes we struggle to use our special skills to help in a particular way. This can hold us back at work. For example, someone who's really good with numbers might work as a waiter in a restaurant. But they don't use their math skills, so they don't stand out.

Helping others is important, but what really matters is using your special skills to achieve a specific goal. I've seen lots of people apply for jobs just because of the title or salary, not because they can use their unique skills in that job.

Did you know you can use your special talents to help without fulfilling your individual purpose? Let's say I'm a marketer at a car company. I'm using my skills to promote cars, but sadly I'm not passionate about cars. I'd rather work at a university, where I can use my skills for a purpose I care about, educating others. When you combine your special gifts with serving the people you really care about, that's when you'll feel the most fulfilled.

5. Purpose Leads to Dream

Purpose is like your life's GPS. It tells you why you're here and what you should do. Without it, you might start one thing today, then something else tomorrow, and keep changing without getting anywhere. You only have 24 hours each day, so not having purpose can mean you waste time on things that don't really matter.

Purpose gives you a clear path. When you have that path, you can start dreaming big. Dreams don't come out of nowhere; they're built on your purpose.

When I was a teenager, I looked up to people like Lionel Messi, the soccer star. I wanted to be like him, but it was just a wish. I hadn't found my purpose. But when I did, it was like turning on a light. I could see exactly who I wanted to be and how to get there.

6. Purpose Reveals Your Strengths (Talents and Skills)

Learning new skills to help others is good, but it's hard to stand out nowadays without knowing your purpose. When you know your purpose, you can focus on learning the right skills for your mission. Some people learn a lot of skills without knowing why. But what's the use of a skill if it doesn't help you with your mission in life?

Sure, knowing different things is useful, but spending too much time on something that doesn't match your purpose is a waste. Imagine spending all your time studying jewellery when your real purpose is to create beautiful songs. People who are pushed or forced into something that doesn't fit their purpose often end up unhappy and sometimes even depressed because they're not doing what really matters to them.

For me, discovering that I was good at communicating was like finding the last piece of a puzzle. Before that, I was learning all sorts of things without a clear reason. But once I understood my purpose, everything clicked into place. I knew what skills and knowledge I needed to make a difference.

I found out that my purpose was all about helping and inspiring others. That's when I realised how crucial communication was. It became like a map for my journey. Every word I said and every message I wrote had a bigger purpose. They were tools to share ideas and make a positive change.

Before, I was learning random things. But now, I focused on getting better at communicating. I studied how to speak persuasively and understand how people feel. Every new skill I learnt felt like a step closer to becoming really good at communicating for my purpose.

This shift made a huge difference. I wasn't

just talking for the sake of it; I was communicating with a clear goal. It felt amazing. I wasn't speaking just to fill the air; I was sharing to help others grow. This changed how I interacted with people and how I saw myself. Communication became a way to live my purpose and truly make a difference.

FINDING YOUR PURPOSE

I studied computer science in college and worked as a web developer for a few years before switching to marketing. While I liked my job, I felt something was missing. It seemed like I had no real reason to wake up each day beyond paying bills and doing what's expected. Have you ever felt like this?

In 2010, I self-published a fantasy book called "ICIRE: The Rebirth." I wrote seven more books afterward, but none of them made me truly happy. People praised me as a prolific writer, but I wasn't satisfied. It wasn't imposter syndrome; I knew I had good stories to tell. But something felt off in the way I was telling them. One big clue was that I didn't enjoy reading creative fiction i.e. fantasy books, yet I was writing them. How did this make sense?

In 2018, I joined a coaching group where we had to read and discuss a book. It had been a while since I'd read a book, but I decided to give it a try. I bought the book and started reading. At first, it felt like a chore, but something changed. I found myself excited to pick up the book during my free time. This hadn't happened in years. What's more, the book was about leadership, a far cry from any of the books I used to read prior. Little did I know, this would lead me to discover my purpose.

After finishing the coaching programme, I decided to explore another non-fiction book, this time about workplace productivity. My passion for reading was reignited, and I started reading everywhere – on buses, trains, even in waiting rooms and bathrooms. I extended my morning time just to read one more chapter, even if it meant feeling a bit tired at work. It felt worth it.

Then, I got invited to another coaching session, this one about testing your dreams. I enjoyed every moment of it and ended up reading more books by the same author. A few months later, I realised I had become a book enthusiast. Every time I went to WH Smith, I headed straight for the book section. In that year, I read more books than I had in my entire life. Some might say that during that first coaching session, something clicked, transforming the way I saw books. I believe I found a passion that began to awaken a desire in me – a desire to teach, coach, and guide others to be their best.

I had discovered a passion for reading non-fiction books that could improve people's lives. My deep desire to see people happy and peaceful made me genuinely appreciate the ideas in these self-help books. However, I hadn't found my purpose yet, not until I held my first seminar. In my local church, I saw a need to help members grow personally. I asked the pastor if I could organise seminars to teach and coach interested members. My first seminar was about using concentration to improve performance and productivity in life. I prepared carefully and presented it to about a dozen people. As the seminar ended, I realised something important: despite feeling tired, I loved every moment and would have done another seminar right away. That's when I discovered my purpose, and it changed my life forever.

How to Find Your Purpose

Everything in existence, including people, has a purpose. But finding your specific purpose can be a challenge. I've looked into many resources and listened to discussions about this.

As a Christian, I have a unique view on discovering purpose. I believe that just like products are made by manufacturers, we humans are created by God. And just as a product's purpose is known through its maker, our individual purposes are revealed with God's guidance. There are two main ways to discover our purpose on Earth.

1. Ask your creator

While you were born to a mother and father, Christians believe that God is your ultimate creator, like a heavenly Father. Parents may have dreams for their children, but they can't fully know their true purpose without God's help. God has given each person unique gifts to fulfil their purpose on Earth, like a manufacturer giving specific features to a product. Parents can help their child discover their purpose by recognising these gifts.

In my upbringing, I always wanted to be someone who could solve problems and make a meaningful impact in the world. I found my true purpose when I embraced Christ and asked God to show it to me. The key is recognising your need for divine guidance and humbly seeking God's help in this journey.

You might be wondering, what about people who don't believe in God but still seem to have found their purpose. Well let's talk about that next step.

2. Unlock the Secrets of the Mind

Think of it like this: just as you might read a manual that comes with a product to understand how it works, you can also uncover your purpose by understanding your gifts, potential, and passions, even if you don't necessary seek a relationship with God. God has placed gifts within each person, and some focus on discovering these gifts to find parts of their purpose.

But here's the difference: if you go with the second approach (discovering your gifts without divine guidance), you might miss out on the full picture of your purpose. Manuals for products can only tell you so much. People who take this path could use their gifts to help others but still struggle with things like depression and anxiety. On the other hand, those who follow the first path by building a relationship with God will continuously learn about their purpose as they go through life's different stages. They'll understand their gifts better and how best to use them, staying true to themselves all the way. And most importantly, they would understand how to show love and help others. The truth is people believe they understand love, but it's when they encounter Christ that they realise they didn't really know how to love the way He did.

A Blend of Art and Science

Discovering your purpose involves both an art and a science. To put it simply, science is meant to be objective and guided by data whereas art is meant to be subjective and guided by emotions and opinions.

The Scientific Approach

There are many ways to learn about your talents and passions. In my book on human identity, I talked about four things that can help you find your talents. These things tell you what makes you special and how to use your unique gifts. But just having these tools might not be enough to find your purpose. This is where the creative part comes in.

The Artistic Approach

Discovering your passion means being open to new experiences. That's why parents let their kids try lots of different things – to find what they're good at. Even if you have tools to find your strengths (the scientific part), trying out different things is also important to really know what you love. I worked in over a dozen jobs before I figured out my passion. I used some methods (the scientific approach) to understand my purpose, but the experiences were just as important. If I only relied on experiences without a strategy, I might not have found my purpose so clearly. Both the strategy and experiences work together to get great results.

There's no one perfect way to discover your purpose. You might find it quickly, or it might take a lot of attempts But the surest way to uncover your purpose is by connecting with the one who made you.

REFLECTION

1. Do you believe in a collective purpose?

2. If you could dedicate your life to solving one problem or making one aspect of the world better, what would it be, and why does this cause resonate with you?

3. Can you recall moments in your life when you felt a strong sense of purpose?

4. Do you believe that you were created for a purpose?

5. Does the idea of purpose affect your daily activities?

PART II

DREAM

WHAT IS NOT A DREAM

When I was 11, I had a big dream. I lived in Nigeria, but in my mind, I was in Hollywood. Every day, I'd imagine myself as a famous rapper and actor, walking down red carpets, and winning Grammy and Academy Awards. It felt amazing. I watched TV shows, music videos, and award ceremonies, practising acceptance speeches in front of my mirror. I could see myself smiling as they called my name for "Best Actor" or "Best Rapper." I imagined walking confidently to the stage, thanking everyone with a microphone in hand. But there was one thing I didn't ask myself back then: "Is this dream what I really want?"

Talking about dreams, it's crucial to know what's a real dream and what's just a wish. Many, like my younger self, mix wishes with real dreams. They forget a crucial question. Let's clear up some misconceptions about what a true dream is.

A dream is not a wish

People sometimes confuse wishes with dreams because both involve using your imagination. Think about the movie Aladdin – in it, a young man finds a magical lamp with a powerful genie inside. This genie can grant three wishes to whoever rubs the lamp. It's so incredible that many people wish they could find such a lamp in real life.

A wish is like wanting something without having to do anything for it. For instance, you might wish to have a fit athlete's body without eating healthy or exercising. Or wish to be the richest person without working hard or having the right mindset.

I used to really want to be a famous actor in Hollywood, but I wasn't willing to do what it takes to make that dream come true. The truth is, being a Hollywood star is a dream, but it turns into a wish when it's not something you're truly committed to. I didn't have the determination, talents, and passion required for that dream. When I realised it wasn't my real dream, I called it a wish and moved on. Sadly, some people keep thinking that what they wish for is their dream, even when they can't actually make it happen.

A dream is not a goal

In life, if you want to achieve something important, you have to set goals. A goal is like the thing you really want to achieve in the future. But it's important to know that goals and dreams are not the same. You achieve goals to make your dream come true, but the goal itself is not the dream.

Sometimes people set goals for the future, but they don't feel motivated or inspired enough to reach them. A dream is like the first step towards creating a goal, and it's something you shouldn't ignore. Many people focus more on setting and reaching their goals because it feels more real than their dream.

Goals usually have a deadline, which is a time when you need to finish them. This is why it's hard to be an entrepreneur because your goals come from your dream. People who work full-time jobs don't have this challenge. Their goals are set by their bosses, based on the big dream or plan the company already has.

Before I knew my purpose and had a

dream, I used to set many goals without having a dream to guide me. I didn't realise that doing this would only work for a short time. I lacked the motivation and direction to reach my goals.

In the past, I set goals because I felt pressure to be important. For example, I saw an ad about making an online store as a business, and I set big goals for it. I did make the store, but then I didn't have the motivation to do the next goal because I didn't have a bigger dream.

Goals have an end point, and without a dream behind them, you can easily get distracted and move to a new goal that has nothing to do with the first one. For instance, I finished the online store and then started writing a book. These two goals were not connected. The people I wanted to help with the online store were different from the people I wanted to help with the book. I got tired and gave up on the online store idea. Looking back, I understand that my goals weren't leading me to the future I wanted because I didn't have a dream.

A dream is not a borrowed idea

Many people begin projects just to impress others. Nowadays, some people want to be entrepreneurs just because their friends are in business. A few years back, I was with some friends, hanging out and having fun, when we got sidetracked by a TV ad. The ad was about a cool new product, maybe a smartwatch, but I don't quite remember. We got talking about starting our own businesses instead of watching the football game. We left that room with plans to start our own businesses. The problem wasn't the ideas we came up with, but the mindset behind them. We all thought we were dreaming big, but sadly, I haven't seen any of those ideas come true, including mine. Why? They came from pressure, seeing an ad, and then we all started talking about great ideas. Maybe a couple of us were truly dreaming, but others might have just been joining in because everyone else was. This is happening more these days with the rise of online businesses. Everyone wants to be a business owner. If you look closely, you'll see they lack the plan or courage to set the right goals to make their ideas real. They're easily influenced by friends or society, chasing goals based on others' dreams. They don't get that the drive to reach certain goals should come from wanting to make their own dreams come to pass.

I had a chance to talk with one of my coaching clients about their dreams. Let's call them Mike for this story. Mike told me he wanted to own property and stocks and work on the designs of his places. I loved the idea and could see him doing all that. A while later, Mike told me he was starting an online business with some friends. He seemed really excited, so I didn't want to bring him down. But I was curious about why he wanted to start an online business. He said he just wanted to make a lot of money and be financially free to do whatever he wanted. That's a good reason, but it's not always strong enough to keep you going when things get tough. It's a broad goal. Mike dropped his dream of owning property and picked up the idea of becoming rich because his friends were doing it. If Mike wanted to help his friends achieve their dreams while also getting ready to build his own dream, I'd be really happy for him. But that's not what happened.

He thought he was chasing a new dream.

Mike isn't alone in this. I was in his shoes a few years ago. I left my full-time job to start a business with someone who inspired me and a team that motivated me. My dream was to create a digital marketing agency that would help small and big businesses market their products or services. It was tough deciding to leave a good-paying job for a new business. But I was excited to work with a team and create something amazing.

A few weeks into my new role as the CEO with a team of 5 members, I started feeling the pressure. In a meeting with the company's co-founder, a new vision was shared. They wanted to build a media production company creating digital creative products like music, books, and artworks. They thought this would allow us to make money even when we're not actively working, unlike the digital marketing agency which traded our time for money. I thought about it and decided to go along, even though it wasn't really my dream. I realised later that I had given up my dream for someone else's without fully understanding it. The new vision wasn't based on my strengths like my original dream. Luckily, I realised this a few months later, quit my role before it was too late.

Does this mean that working for others should be avoided? Definitely not! In reality, being part of someone else's dream, especially as an employee, can be really satisfying. But it's important to know the difference between helping others with their dreams and fully embracing those dreams as your own.Having a job is a chance to use your skills and knowledge to help someone else's vision come true. As an employee, you're a key player in making the whole thing work. This doesn't just give you a sense of achievement and help you grow professionally, but it also contributes to making important goals happen.

However, it's crucial to keep your own dreams separate from the dreams of those you work for. While you might really want to support your employer's goals, it's vital to remember what you want for yourself. You have your own unique talents, passions, and dreams that deserve attention. By understanding this, you can actively chase your own goals while also helping others achieve theirs.

WHAT IS A DREAM?

I was just 13 when I had my first dream. I was in school and always busy with different things. I liked being active. If I wasn't having fun or learning something, I'd be sleeping. I didn't really spend much time thinking. But then something special happened.

It was a regular Saturday afternoon at home. I was watching TV in my room when I heard a knock at the front door. My mum was in the living room, so I figured she'd tell the visitor to come in. I stayed in my room. A little while later, my mum called me because my sister's boyfriend wanted to say hi. My sister was studying in the UK, and I was in Nigeria with my parents. So, I knew her boyfriend must be from the UK.

I went to the living room and saw a young man who looked like the singer Omarion. I was amazed. I could feel my arms getting all tingly and my heart started to race when he spoke with his cool accent. I greeted him and then sat down. He asked me about my dreams. I always wanted to study something related to computers, and he was studying Computing. He also played basketball at his university.

At that moment, I decided I wanted to study abroad too. I spent hours imagining myself in the United States, going to school and playing basketball. I knew my parents couldn't afford to send me abroad, but I had a dream. I believed in it so much that I worked hard to make it come true. Many years later, I'm now working in the United Kingdom, following the completion my bachelor's and master's degrees. What felt like just a dream back then turned out to be the beginning of something amazing.

It starts with a dream. I believe you need to imagine something in your mind before you can do something really amazing. In the last chapter, I shared a few misconceptions surrounding the concept of dreaming. I mentioned this because I don't want you to spend a lot of time going after something that looks like a dream but isn't really one, or maybe it's not the right one for you.

Now, let's look into what a dream is and why it's really important to have one.

The Meaning of a Dream

What do you think of when you hear the words "your dream"? Do you imagine what happens when you sleep at night? Or do you think about the person you want to be in the future? A dream can mean one of these things, or maybe both. But we're not going to talk about the sleeping kind of dreams. So don't mix up the dreams you have at night with the ones that come from your purpose.

To be completely honest, there are numerous definitions on the Internet, but the one that really stuck with me was given by John C. Maxwell. He defined a dream as an image and blueprint of a person's purpose and potential. Isn't that interesting? A dream isn't just an image, it's also a blueprint.

As an Image

A dream is like a picture of who you want to be when you grow up. It's like an idea that stays in your mind as you figure out what you're meant to do and start doing it. A dream uses your imagination to show you a picture that makes you want to do things.

You don't need to take special classes or finish school to have a dream. Anyone can dream. The problem is that some people aren't encouraged to dream. So they spend their days working hard just to get by. If you ask them where they want to be in 20 years, they might not know because they haven't been shown how to imagine it. That's why it's good for kids to do different activities at school, home, church etc. It helps them see they can dream. It's tough to dream if you're always around people who don't inspire you to dream.

As a blueprint

A dream isn't only a picture in your mind. It can also give you hints on how to make it happen if you think about it a lot. Some folks might have started dreaming, but they got sidetracked by life's challenges and let their dream fade away. If all you can see is a future version of you, then it might not be your dream. It could be more like a wish, like we talked about earlier.

A dream shows you a plan for turning the picture in your mind into real life. Like in my story, I had a dream to study abroad. I could imagine myself walking in American colleges. But it didn't stop there, I got brave enough to take steps to make it come true. Your dream will make you really curious and aware. You'll start looking for ways to make it real. If you don't feel driven to find a way to reach your dream, then maybe it wasn't your. dream after all.

Everyone can dream. But not everyone does, and some who dream don't make their dreams real. Here are a few reasons why I believe having a dream is so important:

A dream gives you direction

When I had the dream of pursuing higher education, it pointed me in the right direction. I could have chosen different paths, just to have backup plans. However, that would have brought distractions and uncertainties. I knew where I had to go and couldn't waste time on things that wouldn't bring me closer to my dream. I remember taking the SATs, an international exam that would qualify me for a university programme in the US. But that wasn't all – I also decided to study Cambridge A Levels for a chance to go to a UK university.

Some of my friends didn't understand why I was taking those paths, but I had a dream. A dream that pushed me to take bold steps toward a specific goal.

Without a clear idea of where you want to go in life, you might end up just following what others are doing or simply going with the first opportunity that comes your way. A dream gives you a sense of direction by showing you a glimpse of your future self. Once you can imagine who you could become, the next step is figuring out how to make it happen. Sometimes people get caught up doing what society expects, even if it doesn't align with their true purpose. For example, you might have the potential to become a fantastic musician who brings joy to the world, but societal pressures might push you to settle for being an "average" accountant.

A Dream Inspires Action

Once you can see, you can take action. It doesn't matter how small that action is; having a dream motivates you to take the first step. Often, people come up with ideas for how they want to live their lives, but they get stuck in the planning stage. They lack the energy to figure out how to begin. Someone with a dream finds the necessary energy to work toward a future they desire. It's feasible that a person with a dream can have a full-time job and still find time to build their business. People might wonder where this person gets the energy, especially after a long workday. Their energy comes from their dream. We all need a dream to guide us in doing things that bring happiness and joy to our lives.

A person with a dream understands that their dream depends on time to become real. They don't just wait for everything to be perfect before taking action. Even if it means brainstorming ideas to solve a problem, saving money to buy a property to let, or reading books for inspiration to write your next book, a dream empowers you to start the journey from where you are and with what you have.

A dream creates worthy goals

Anyone has the ability to set a goal and reach it. However, this doesn't necessarily mean they will find fulfilment. They might only experience the result of completing a task, essentially finishing what they started. A goal on its own isn't valuable without a supporting dream. It's not advisable to create ambitious goals without a solid foundation. Once you have a dream, it becomes simpler to define the appropriate goals that will bring that dream to life. Your dream doesn't always have to revolve around your career; it could encompass your well-being, family, or spiritual journey.

Goals empower us to accomplish significant things, but they hold little value if they don't contribute to our physical, mental, spiritual, and emotional growth. This is why some individuals invest excessive time in activities that fail to provide true satisfaction. They prefer being occupied rather than being effective. The reason certain people prioritise wealth over family is often due to a lack of vision for their relationships. They might envision financial success but not a harmonious personal life. It's crucial to have a comprehensive dream that encompasses all aspects of life: health, wealth, relationships, and spirituality.

A dream helps overcome obstacles

In life, there are some things you can count on, like facing obstacles when you start a journey. When you're working to make a great life for your family, challenges will come that might make you want to give up. But if you have a clear vision i.e. a dream, you can find different ways to overcome these challenges. Keep in mind that your dream could stay the same, but how you get there might need to change. So, having a vision is like having the tools to make the right changes to reach your desired end.

Teaching has always been my passion. Even back when I was a student, I enjoyed teaching my classmates about subjects I loved. But due to a health condition, I couldn't become a full-time teacher. So, I found different ways to make my teaching dream come true. Now, I lead workshops, seminars, and teach at my church. My career goal remains the same, but the paths I take to get there have changed. If you have a clear vision, you're not too worried about the different routes you might need to take. The main thing is realising your dream.

As I mentioned earlier, my initial dream wasn't specifically about studying in the US; it was more about studying in a developed country. So, when I got the chance to study in the UK, I didn't turn it down just because it wasn't the US. I stayed flexible and kept pursuing my dream, knowing that the path might look different from what I expected, but it would still lead to the same goal.

I've learnt that some people fail to reach their goals because they don't have a clear vision. When they face an obstacle, they lose hope because they think there's no other way to reach that particular goal.

DREAMS AND ROLE MODEL

When I was younger, my big brother was my role model, especially during my time in secondary school. My dad was in the military and often had to go to different cities, so I didn't have another male figure to look up to except my brother. He was really smart, had a great reputation. He even became the "Head Boy" at our school, sort of like the leader. Even though I didn't say it out loud, I secretly wanted to be like him. Sometimes, teachers would say, "Why can't you be more like your brother?" and I'd wonder, "Haven't I asked myself the same thing?"

He not only did well in school but also didn't argue much with our parents. He was quiet, which made our parents like him more. I knew they loved me, but it was clear they liked him better. So, I wanted to be like him to get people to like me more too. Basically, I wanted to copy his personality.

Honestly, I didn't have anyone else to look

up to besides my family. I wasn't into comics or superheroes, even though I watched a lot of movies. I'd watch the films but then forget about them and go back to my normal life. I didn't take the time to think about what the superheroes stood for or how they could teach me something valuable. It was all just entertainment.

One day, something amazing happened when I met my sister's boyfriend at our house. It gave me a new kind of inspiration. Even though I didn't really understand what a "role model" was back then, I looked up to this person and used their influence to work towards my dream. If it wasn't for that meeting on that sunny day in my parents' living room, I might not have been willing to move to the UK. Meeting him didn't just give me a dream; it also connected me with someone who had already achieved what I wanted to do. Even though we had different paths, I could learn from his experiences to make smart choices on my journey. Role models are really important when you're chasing your dreams.

After talking to many people and doing a lot of research about role models, I found some common reasons why people struggle to find their own role models.

The Concept of Being Self-Made

Some people believe they can succeed all on their own, without needing help or guidance from others. In the past, it was rare for someone from a disadvantaged background to become successful. But in today's world, many people who started with very little have become financially secure. This has led some to think they don't need role models to achieve their dreams.

These people are convinced that sheer hard work and determination are enough to make them successful. They don't like taking advice from others, even if those others are highly respected. They prefer to learn from their own mistakes and don't want to credit anyone else for their success. If you look closely, you might notice a bit of pride in the way they carry themselves. They struggle with the idea of following someone else's path, and eventually, they wonder why they're not leading a fulfilling and enriched life.

In talent competitions like singing, judges

often ask contestants who they want to be like if they win. Those who believe in being entirely self-made might say, "I don't want to be like anyone else." They don't realise that having a role model doesn't take away from their unique abilities; it actually adds depth and grace to their talents.

Limited Access

We all know that where you live can greatly affect how successful you become. Many people have come to the United Kingdom, hoping for a better life and more opportunities. But some folks aren't lucky enough to be near successful people they can look up to. They might start thinking they can't have a role model because they grew up in a tough place with no one to guide them. While there's some truth to this, I believe it's a limiting idea. You don't have to be close to great people from the start to begin your journey. There are lots of life-changing books, videos, documentaries, and more that can introduce you to role models who can change your life. Don't let limited access be an excuse to narrow your dream.

As I write this book, I don't have John Maxwell's phone number or email address, but that doesn't mean he can't be one of my role models. I don't need to call him to learn from his experiences.

Yearning for Originality

Many people struggle with the idea of having role models because they worry it might make them less unique. They avoid creating anything similar to what's already out there. They don't want to learn from others who've done what they want to do. Instead, they're always looking for completely new ideas that no one has thought of before. They spend years trying to create something entirely fresh instead of using what others have already done as a starting point. This kind of person wants to be a pioneer in their field. But they don't realise that they can still be trailblazers while having role models. If you're like this, I encourage you to change your thinking. Role models are there to set standards that you can aim to exceed.

WHY ARE ROLE MODELS IMPORTANT?

Awareness

For the longest time, I never thought about improving myself until I read a book by John C. Maxwell. It changed my life by helping me understand my purpose, talents, and potential. Without self-help books, I might never have discovered my passion for writing books that transform lives.

When you engage with the work of your role model, it brings a level of awareness. It ignites something inside you and makes you think about following a similar path. For instance, Neil Armstrong, the first person on the moon, got his passion for flying when he was just six years old during a plane ride. This led him to become a pilot and later an astronaut. It's worth noting that he wasn't the only one on that flight, but something about flying sparked his passion. Without pilots as role models, his breakthrough might not have happened. Role models show us many possibilities in life.

Wisdom

There are times when just being aware of something isn't enough to turn your passion into something successful. You need insights, lessons, and real-life examples to give you the wisdom to navigate your path. Some may wonder, "How can we connect with our role models, especially if they're famous like Michelle Obama?" This is where autobiographies and interviews come in. Many influential people write books about their lives, and these books help you understand their challenges, strengths, and what they've learnt.

Even though I haven't met John C. Maxwell in person, I've spent time listening to his teachings and interviews. From this, I learnt that he was a pastor before becoming a leadership expert, speaker, and author. I got insights into his mistakes, habits, and opportunities, which now help me with my own goals. While I may not follow his exact path, I have the resources to reach a similar destination. Role models can provide the wisdom you need for your journey. Success leaves clues, and by studying your role model's life, you can gain valuable tools to improve your own journey.

Inspiration

A role model can bring out the greatness within you. Sometimes, you might doubt how much you can achieve with your talents. A role model can inspire you by showing what they've accomplished. Take John C. Maxwell, for instance. He's written more than 80 books, and that motivates me to write more, not to compete, but to be inspired and realise my potential. Even if I don't reach that exact milestone, I'll still write more books than I would without a role model.

One amazing thing about living role models is seeing them set new records. It's not about competing with them, but getting excited by their achievements, which encourages you to keep going in your own pursuits. When I see my role models speaking to thousands in a stadium, it inspires me. I can imagine myself doing that someday.

But remember, don't turn your role model into an idol. They're there to help you grow, but don't focus so much on their journey that you neglect your own. If you're a writer and you're reading all your role model's books, make sure you also spend time writing your own. Role models guide you, but it's up to you to put in the work to make your dreams come true.

QUALIFYING YOUR DREAM

In today's world, with lots of online info and social media, it's easy to think someone else's dream is yours. You might see a video on Instagram of someone you follow performing on stage and think, "I could do that too." You start talking about your dream to perform on stage.

But how can you be sure this dream is really yours? How can you avoid spending time on a dream that's not even yours? You need to learn how to check if your dream is real. You should have some confidence that it's truly yours.

A while back, I found a great book by John C. Maxwell called "Put Your Dream to the Test." In it, he lists 10 questions you should ask to be sure about your dreams. In this chapter, I'll share those 10 things to help you know if your dreams are right for you.

The Ownership Check

Do you realise you can chase a dream that's not really yours? Can you be sure the dream you're holding is truly meant for you? Are you using your special skills for this dream, or are you relying on others to make it happen? Maybe you're so focused on the end result that you're missing the necessary steps to achieve it.

Think about this: you see a speaker in front of a huge crowd, and it makes you want to be a speaker too. But are you ready to put in the work to become an effective speaker for such a big audience? I often tell young professionals to pay more attention to a job's responsibilities in a job ad rather than just the benefits. If you can do all the listed tasks well, you'll likely get rewarded. This advice helps people choose jobs that match their skills instead of just chasing material things. The same goes for your dream – make sure it passes the ownership check.

The Clarity Check

Once you're sure the dream is truly yours, the next step is to make it clear and easy to understand, both for yourself and others. If your dream is fuzzy, it's hard to know how to work toward it. When I work as a coach, I help young adults make their dreams clear. I've seen that without this, many won't take the steps needed to make their dreams real.

Being clear doesn't mean you need to plan every little detail. It means you should have a clear idea at the core. If you can't explain your dream in a way that others can understand, it lacks clarity. Even if people don't agree with your dream, they should be able to get what it is. Sadly, lots of people go through life without a clear and exciting vision of their dream. I think if you can't picture your dream, it's hard to make the right plan to achieve it. Writing this book (and my last three) would've been tough if I didn't understand my dream clearly.

The Reality Check

Thinking you can achieve any dream just by wanting it isn't smart. Wishing for a dream doesn't mean it will happen. It takes more than that. When I was a teenager, I wanted to be the best football player in school. But I had to face the truth. Even though I really wanted it,

I didn't have the talent or skills to make it happen.

Dreaming something that depends on other people's abilities isn't a good idea. I've seen many people daydream about things that have nothing to do with what they're good at. Maybe you've watched a famous athlete win a trophy, and you start dreaming that you'll do it too. But if your dream relies on things you can't control, you're just wasting your time.

The Passion Check

I used to think passion meant just liking something, but now I see it differently. Passion means being ready to face tough times for what you love. Are you willing to go through hard situations to make your dream real? Passion gives you the energy to work on your business even when you're tired after a long day. You're ready to handle stress in the short term to help your business grow. Sadly, many people try to start a side business but can't make it work because they don't pick something they're really passionate about.

In simple words, if you're not ready to face difficulties for it, you won't achieve your dream. Hard times, problems, letdowns, and challenges will come up while you're chasing your dream. Passion gives you the strength to get through these tough times and keeps your dream alive.

The Plan Check

There's a famous saying: "if you fail to plan, you plan to fail." This applies to chasing your dream too. You can't just sit at home waiting for luck. You need a plan, a strategy. Even if someone is interested in supporting you, it won't work without a plan. A plan tells you what to do. Without it, you might be stuck, dreaming but not moving forward.

Making a plan is important, but many people stop there. The real power is in doing what your plan says. You can't achieve your dream without taking action. For example, my plan as a writer is to write a dozen books by my 35th birthday. It's a good plan, but if I don't write every day, it won't happen. So, having a plan is not enough; you must do what it says.

The Team Check

You can't do big things without people. Whether you want to start a business or move up in a job, you need to work with others. If you can't get along with people, reaching your dream will be hard. That's why I don't like the term "self-made." Nobody does it all alone. To reach your dream, you need help from others. The bigger your dream, the more help you'll need.

Your dream depends on having the right team to help you succeed. That's why it's important to choose the right person to share your life with, your spouse. In recent years, I've been able to work long hours each week because my wife believes in my dream and supports me every day. It would be tough to navigate the challenges of running a business if I had problems at home. Some people focus on building a great team at work but forget about the even more important team at home. Don't go through life alone, especially if you want to reach your dream. You need people, and people need you.

The Price Check

Are you ready to do what it takes to make your dream real? Almost everyone who's achieved something big had to make sacrifices. I saw how hard my parents worked to get where they did in their jobs when I was growing up.

Take Soyin Sobowale, a famous Nigerian actress. She was doing really well in Nigeria, but she left her career to move to London and take care of her kids. She had to do low-paying jobs just to get by. Not every mom would do that, but she had a dream about raising her kids a certain way, and she was willing to do whatever it took to make it happen.

So, at some point, you'll have to decide if you're ready to pay the price to make your dream come true. But here's the thing, not every dream is worth chasing. Some dreams might end up hurting you, especially if you haven't built the right values and character. You could become a famous actor but lose your family in the process. So, was it worth it? Don't pay a price you can't afford.

Before you dive in, do some research. See what sacrifices others in your field had to make to get where they are. For example, if you want to be a global music star, you'll have to travel a lot for concerts. Even in the digital age, touring is a big deal for artists. If you want fame but don't want to leave your hometown, you won't get there. Why? Because you're not ready to pay the price.

The Tenacity Check

Throughout history, we've seen that people who chase their dreams share some common qualities. One of these is called "tenacity," which is like not giving up, even when things are super hard. I'm really interested in athletes and entrepreneurs. Imagine an athlete preparing for the Olympics. They wake up early every day, no matter if it's sunny or rainy, and practise for hours. Some days, they feel super tired and like they can't win, but they don't stop. They keep going because they really want to stand on that podium with a medal around their neck.

Successful business people also face lots of problems while trying to make their dream business work. Sometimes their business doesn't do as well as they hoped, or they run out of money, or there's a lot of competition. But they don't give up. They change their plans, learn from their mistakes, and keep moving forward because they really believe in their dream of having a successful business.

This thing called tenacity is what makes dreamers different from people who only dream but don't achieve. It's about being ready to face tough times, adapt to change, and not give up, which is what helps you achieve your dreams. So, when life gets tough while you're chasing your dreams, remember how important it is to be tenacious. Face the challenges, learn from them, and keep taking small, steady steps forward because that's where the real power to achieve your dreams comes from.

Think of tenacity as a secret superpower. It's what keeps you going even when others might stop trying. It's your strong determination to reach your dreams, no matter how hard the journey gets. It's like the fuel that pushes your dream forward.

Being tenacious doesn't mean you won't face problems or failures along the way. Actually, it's the opposite. Being tenacious means you face those problems head-on and use them to get closer to your big goal. When you see obstacles, you don't think of them as roadblocks. Instead, you see them as chances to learn, grow, and become even stronger.

So, as you work towards your dreams, don't forget the power of tenacity. Keep that strong desire inside you, and don't let difficulties stop you. Stick to your dream, adjust when needed, and keep taking those small, steady steps forward. With tenacity on your side, you have the special sauce to make your dreams come true.

The Satisfaction Check

I remember the year I worked as a web developer at a college in the UK. My job was to create an online system for students and teachers to track results. It's one of my favourite work memories. You know why? Because I found more happiness in the work itself than in the final result. Every time I completed a part of the project, I felt really happy. Back then, I enjoyed the journey of working on it, not just the end goal. This same idea should apply to your dream.

Your dream isn't only about getting to the

finish line. It's also about the journey you take to get there. Even if you don't reach your ultimate goal, you can still feel fulfilled along the way. If you're chasing a dream that doesn't bring you any satisfaction, maybe it's time to think about a different path. I'm not saying your dream journey will be easy; it will have tough and unexpected atimes. But the journey should still make you feel good and keep you motivated. I've often wondered why some really exceptional people keep facing tough challenges. They don't give up because they find fulfilment in chasing their dream, and you should too.

The Significance Check

After talking to many people with dreams, it's surprising to see some only chasing dreams that benefit themselves. Tony Robbins often talks about how his mission is to make life better. He didn't start his journey just to get rich or collect money without doing anything. Instead, he focused on helping and improving others. This might sound simple, but many people only think about what they can get from their dreams and forget how they could help others.

This last point is really important. You can't underestimate how powerful it is to give something valuable to others. Almost all successful people have made giving value to others a big part of their journey to achieve their dreams. Even people who work alone, like basketball players, spend extra time training to make sure they bring value to their team and fans. If your dream doesn't inspire you to help others, it's time to rethink that dream.

REFLECTION

1. Do you have a dream? If yes, how did you receive or realise it?

2. Have you ever chased something you thought was a dream but wasn't yours to pursue?

3. Do you believe in role models? Do you have any?

4. Have you been discouraged to dream?

5. Where do you see yourself in 20 years from reading this book?

PART III

TALENT

INTRODUCTION TO TALENTS

Understanding your talents can be tough. We often follow the usual path and don't spend time discovering what makes us unique. We finish school without fully knowing why we like certain subjects. Some people go to college without understanding their strengths and weaknesses. It's easier to do what feels good than to figure out why it feels that way. By the end of this part, I want you to have a better idea of your talents and how you can use them to make the world better.

Many books talk about how hard work and discipline lead to success. But we hear more about gaining skills than finding our natural talents. Skills are important, but it's not smart to ignore your own talents while learning other skills that make you valuable. No matter how many skills or knowledge you have, true happiness and satisfaction come from using your talents. So, what's a talent?

A talent is something you do or think in a

certain way over and over again, and it's useful. It's not something that happens now and then; it's consistent. Talents come from your mind; you don't learn them from outside. They are rooted in how you think, feel, or act. A talent is real when you can use it effectively in real life. Take curiosity, for example. It's a talent because it can be useful in many fields like journalism, law, science, or writing. If it had no practical use, it wouldn't be a talent.

This leads us to the question of where talents come from. Are talents something you're born with, or do you develop them as you grow? According to Donald Clifton, who led the Gallup International Research & Education Centre, talents are something you're born with, and they become stronger as you get older. When you're a baby, you have billions of brain cells, also known as neurons. These brain cells make connections called synapses, which allow them to communicate. Over time, some brain cells and connections are lost, but specific connections (synapses) become stronger. These synapses weave together as you grow from a baby into a teenager, forming what we call talents.

When I was in high school, I was really

good at math compared to other subjects. I found it easy to learn and even teach my classmates, and I didn't need to study a lot to get top grades. For a long time, I didn't think much about my math abilities, even when I studied computer science in university. I had seen people with unique talents, but I didn't see myself as someone with anything special to offer. I admired football players, musicians, actors, lawyers, and military professionals. But math was the one area where I excelled, and it wasn't until later that I realised I could use my 'problem-solving' talent in the real world.

Benefits of Talents

Hidden within each of us is something special called talent. It's like a gift that can change our lives in big ways. Think of it as a unique spark that makes us different from everyone else, like a fingerprint on the world. When we understand and take care of our talents, they can bring many good things, not just to us but also to the people around us and the whole world.

Talents aren't just about being good at stuff; they're like natural abilities that come from inside us. They're like tiny seeds of our potential that can grow into something amazing. It could be a talent for making art, solving hard problems, connecting with others, or something else special. These talents can open up a lot of opportunities for us.

Let's take a look at some of the benefits of having talents.

Sets You Apart

Your brain is wired in a special way that makes you think, feel, and decide things uniquely. This is why it's important to understand your talents if you want to make a difference in the world. Even if you're studying or working in a similar field as others, the way you do things will be different. Your talents make you approach things in your way because they're based on how your mind works.

Some folks focus a lot on learning new skills, but they forget about their talents. This can lead them to do just okay in their jobs or classes. For example, when I was in university, I was decent at computer programming - I'd say I was "above average," but not the best. After I graduated, I realised this and decided to try something else where I could really shine. It took me more than ten years to figure out my talents and how to turn them into strengths. Along the way, I found that standing out comes from doing things that use my talents, not just my knowledge or skills.

I sincerely believe your talent can add something fresh to a situation. For instance, at work, I offered to help my boss publish his first book because I knew I had a particular talent that could be useful to him. I didn't get paid for it, and he didn't ask me to do it. I just wanted to contribute in a way that was uniquely mine.

Your talent is a valuable quality that can help you stand out in different ways. It can give you a sense of purpose and direction, making you more valuable in your work or studies.

Discovering Your Life Purpose

Talent is a natural skill or ability you have, and it can help you find your life's purpose. Figuring out your purpose can be tricky, but your talent can guide you in discovering what truly excites you and where you are strong.

Your talent can assist in uncovering your purpose by showing you a clear path. Often, a talent naturally points you toward a particular area or activity. For instance, if you're great at music, your purpose might be to become a musician. Similarly, if math comes easily to you, your purpose could involve becoming a mathematician. This direction focuses your efforts and energy on achieving your goals. It also helps you make decisions about your career, education, and other life choices.

Additionally, your talent contributes to finding your purpose by giving you a sense of fulfilment. When you use your talent to create or help others, you feel satisfied and accomplished. This drive encourages you to keep pursuing your talent, making it a significant part of your life's purpose. This fulfilment deepens your understanding of your values and priorities and how they match your talent. For example, someone talented at teaching might realise their purpose is to be an educator and positively impact others' lives.

Furthermore, your talent can boost your confidence and self-esteem. When you have a talent and do well at it, you often feel proud and valuable. This can lead to better self-awareness and a clearer understanding of your strengths and weaknesses. Such self-awareness helps you make important life choices and set goals that align with your purpose. For instance, someone talented at public speaking might discover their purpose in motivating others as a speaker, inspiring them to achieve their goals.

However, it's essential to know that having talent alone isn't enough to find your purpose. You also need insight from the creator, good self-awareness, a willingness to try new things, and a dedication to growing as a person. While your talent is helpful in uncovering your purpose, it should go along with thinking about yourself, trying out different things, and working hard.

Enhances the Community

Talent isn't just for your benefit; it can also help your community. Talented people have unique skills that can make their community better. Here are some ways your talent can help your community:

Firstly, your talent can be used to meet the needs of your community. For example, a skilled doctor can help people who don't have good access to medical care. A talented teacher can educate and inspire children who come from families with less money. Also, a capable engineer can design things like clean water or electricity systems that help the community.

Secondly, your talent can be used to create and support community projects. For instance, a gifted artist can make beautiful public art that improves the community's look. A skilled businessperson can create jobs and help the community's economy grow. And a talented organiser can bring people together to work on things like making the community more Eco-friendly.

Thirdly, your talent can help motivate and strengthen others in the community. For example, a skilled athlete can use their abilities to encourage young people to stay active and healthy. A talented businessperson can teach others how to start and run their own businesses. Also, a capable public speaker can use their skills to talk about important social and political issues and inspire others to take action.

Lastly, your talent can create a sense of

togetherness and belonging. For instance, a gifted musician can bring people together through music and shared experiences. A skilled chef can use their abilities to build a sense of community through group meals and gatherings. Also, a talented designer can create spaces and environments that make it easier for people to connect and interact.

I strongly believe that your talent can be a powerful tool for making your community better. Talented people i.e. people who have discovered their talents have special skills that can be used to meet community needs, start and support community projects, motivate and empower others, and create a sense of togetherness. It's important for individuals to use their talents to make a positive impact on the community, and for organisations and community leaders to recognise and support the talents of community members to build a stronger, more sustainable, and resilient community.

MISCONCEPTIONS OF TALENTS

"Talent" is a word we often hear, but not everyone truly understands what it means. I've talked to many smart people about talent, and I've heard some different ideas. In this chapter, I'll tell you about some common misunderstandings about talent. I hope you won't let these misunderstandings get in the way of finding and using your talents.

Talents Are Fixed and Unchangeable

Many people mistakenly think that talents are fixed, unchangeable traits that can't be developed. They believe that if they haven't discovered a talent when they were young, it's too late to learn one. But this idea ignores the incredible flexibility of our brains, known as neuroplasticity, and the potential for growth and change. While we might have some natural tendencies, talents can be nurtured and improved through focused practice, ongoing learning, and hard work.

Let's look at Vera Wang's story as an example. She's a famous fashion designer known worldwide. But her path to success was far from simple. When she was young, she was really good at figure skating. She trained hard and even made it onto the U.S. Figure Skating Team. She dreamed of going to the Olympics, but she didn't make it. It was a big setback for her.

However, Vera Wang didn't give up. She decided to try something completely different - fashion, even though she didn't think it was her "talent" before. She started from scratch, working really hard. She learned everything about design, fabrics, and how to create beautiful clothes. Her journey to becoming a famous fashion designer shows us that with effort and a willingness to change, you can transform and discover new talents.

Vera Wang's story boldly challenges the idea that talents are fixed and unchangeable. Even though she was great at figure skating, she took a different path to success. Her story shows that while we might have some natural talents, what really matters is our determination to develop them.

Everyone can learn important lessons from Vera Wang's journey. Our brains can adapt and keep learning throughout our lives. Some folks might naturally be good at certain things, but we all have the potential to grow, learn, and even discover new talents. Age and what we think we know shouldn't limit us. Vera Wang's story tells us that the application of our talents can change and develop. This means that at any point in life, we can start exploring new things, trying new interests, or getting better at skills we never thought we had.

Talents Are Limited To A Group of People

Many people mistakenly think that talent is something only a few lucky folks have, and the rest of us are just ordinary. This idea can make us feel like we don't have any special abilities. But the truth is, everyone has some talent waiting to be found and nurtured.

It's easy to fall into the trap of thinking that only a lucky few have real talent. I used to think this way too. I would look at people who could sing beautifully, paint amazing pictures, or do incredible things in sports, and I'd feel like I didn't measure up. I believed that if I didn't have a talent that was super obvious, there was something wrong with me.

But then I learnt more about what talent really means. I realised that while some talents are easy to see, others are more hidden. Talents can take all sorts of shapes, from being great at connecting with people to being a problem-solver. I found out that my talent for organising and bringing people together was a talent too, even if it wasn't as flashy as some others.

Every person has their unique and valuable talents. Even if a talent isn't obvious at first, it doesn't make it any less important. Consider Albert Einstein, one of the greatest physicists ever. In his early years, he faced problems in school and was seen as slow. But when he followed his love for physics, his incredible talent for creative thinking and problem-solving shone through. His groundbreaking ideas changed how we see the universe.

Thinking that only a few have special talents holds us back. It stops us from finding and developing our own unique skills. We should embrace the idea that talents can be all sorts of things. Discovering these hidden talents is like finding treasures within ourselves. It means knowing that every person has something valuable to offer. When we let go of the idea that only a special group has talent, we empower ourselves to find our unique gifts and make a real difference in the world.

Talent Guarantees Success

Many think having a talent guarantees success. They believe that being exceptionally good at something is enough for excellence in any field. But the truth is more complex. While talent is important, it's not the only thing that decides success.

Think of talent as raw potential. It's like having a block of marble for a sculptor. The sculptor's skill, patience, and effort turn that raw material into a masterpiece. Similarly, a talented person has natural ability, but success needs more.

Success comes from hard work and dedication. It means setting goals, facing challenges, and always getting better. Even if you're talented, reaching the top requires ongoing effort. Just like a gifted athlete combines their natural talent with years of training, pushing their limits, and overcoming obstacles to win.

Success isn't just about finishing tasks; it's also about having specific qualities. Traits like being strong in tough times, staying determined, being humble, and understanding others are equally important. For example, a talented artist can create amazing art, but their ability to handle criticism, learn from mistakes, and work with others helps them achieve long-lasting success.

In reality, success is a mix of talent, continuous effort, and personal growth. It's not a straightforward path; it's a complex mix of factors. While talent can open doors, it's the hard work—the hours spent practising, overcoming self-doubt, and always learning—that leads to victory.

In a world that often wants quick rewards, it's important to say that talent alone doesn't guarantee success. Real success comes from combining talent with hard work, skill with resilience, dedication with character. True success isn't a shortcut; it's a journey that needs ongoing, purposeful effort, driven by a passion to reach your full potential.

Talents Are Limited to Physical Abilities

Another mistaken idea is that talents are only about a person's physical abilities or qualities you can see. This idea makes talents seem like they're only about specific skills that you can show with your body. But talents are much wider than that; they also include things like how you think, feel, and understand.

Here's a story that shows this: There was a famous surgeon known for his amazing surgical skills, especially his ability to use his hands very precisely. But then, something terrible happened, and he couldn't use his hands anymore. It seemed like he had lost his talent.

At first, he was very sad about losing his talent, but he started to discover something important. He realised that his talent wasn't just about his hands; it was also about how well he knew surgery, how smart he was in figuring things out, and how he could lead medical teams. So, his real talent was not only in his hands but also in his interpretation of the medical world and how much he cared about his patients' health.

Undeterred by the problem, the surgeon

found a new way to use his skills. He began to review surgeries, study the best methods, and shared helpful ideas to improve medical procedures. Even though he couldn't use his hands the way he used to, his talent for thinking critically and his dedication to helping patients stayed strong.

This story teaches us an important lesson: talents are not limited by physical abilities. While some talents are easy to see, like being good with your hands, talents can also be about things you can't touch, like problem-solving, caring for others, communicating well, or thinking strategically. These qualities are just as important and can be developed to make a real difference in whatever you choose to do.

The surgeon's story shows that talents can be flexible and adaptable. Just like the surgeon found new ways to use their talents, anyone can explore different aspects of their abilities and qualities. This way of thinking challenges the idea that talents are only about physical skills and encourages people to recognise the many talents they have inside. It reminds us that even if things change, the core qualities that make up our talents are always there, ready to grow and help us succeed.

IDENTIFYING YOUR TALENT

Now that we've talked about why talents are good and cleared up some wrong ideas, let's figure out how to find your own talents. It might surprise you, but many people haven't discovered their talents, so they end up in jobs just to make money.

In this chapter, I'm going to give you four important indicators that can help you find your talents. It might seem tough to figure out what you're really good at, but with the right method, you can discover your unique abilities that make you special.

Here are some things you can do to find your talents:

Reflect on your past experiences and achievements.

Think back on your past and the things you've achieved. This can help you find your talents. It might seem hard, but it's important to understand what makes you happy and successful. One way to find your talents is by looking at what you've done and what you've learnt.

Start by thinking about your past experiences. What have you done that made you happy? What are you good at? What things have always interested you? These experiences can give you clues about your talents and the things you love. For example, if you've always enjoyed writing, you might have a talent for it. If you're good at math, you might be great at solving problems.

Next, think about what you know a lot about. What subjects are you really knowledgeable about? What topics do you find fascinating? What have you studied or learnt about? Your knowledge can also show you your talents. If you know a ton about a certain subject, you might have a talent for it. If you're really interested in something, it could mean you have a natural aptitude in that area.

Now, let's look for patterns in what you've discovered. Are there things that keep coming up in your experiences and knowledge? For example, if you've been really into music for a long time and enjoy it a lot, it might mean you have a talent for music. Or if you know a ton about science and really like it, you might have a talent for science.

Also, think about what other people have told you. Have they said you're good at something? Have they noticed your achievements in a certain area? This feedback is important because it comes from people who have seen what you can do and can give you an honest opinion. Sometimes, they might see talents in you that you didn't notice yourself.

Pay attention to what comes naturally to you.

Often, our talents are things we can do easily and happily. They're the things that feel like we were born to do them. Have you ever wondered why you were really good at some school subjects? Think about Gary Vaynerchuk. He wasn't super great at school subjects, but he was amazing at selling things from a very young age. It just came naturally to him.

In my case, I wasn't a school writing genius. I didn't love literature that much. But I enjoyed writing. Putting my thoughts and ideas on paper was something I liked. I'd write letters to my friends and even made up 'love songs' for my high school crush. Why? Because writing was easy for me. It was simpler to write down what I thought than to say it out loud to someone.

Back in school, there were people who didn't get top grades but could easily speak many languages. On the other hand, some people discovered they were really good at sports like football, basketball, or tennis. These activities just came naturally to them.

Think back to your life, especially when you were growing up. Are there things you were really good at without even trying hard? Sometimes, we don't pay much attention to these things because they seem simple. But if you look closely, you might find your talents. Some folks can cook a great meal without a recipe; it just comes naturally to them. What's your version of that? What do you do easily? You could also talk to your siblings, parents, or anyone you grew up with, especially if they're older. They might remember things you were good at.

If you're a parent trying to find your child's

talent, watch what they're good at in school or other activities. Sometimes, parents focus too much on their child's weaknesses instead of their strengths. It's okay to work on weaknesses, but it's smart to build on strengths.

And don't think your talent is not important just because it's not as famous as other people's talents. For example, maybe you're really good at writing. But if social media likes videos and pictures more, you might think your talent isn't worth much. Don't let what's popular in the media decide how valuable your talents are. Your natural skills are important no matter what's trending.

Explore new activities and hobbies

Trying something new can help you find hidden talents and things you really enjoy. You could start a new hobby or do volunteer work for causes you care about. You might discover something you're good at and love, something you might never find if you don't try. As you get older, it might seem harder to try new things, but don't let that stop you, especially if you haven't found your talent yet.

In an ideal world, parents would introduce

their kids to lots of different things when they're young. But life isn't always ideal, and parents might not have the time or money for extra activities. But that doesn't mean you can't find your talent. Your talent is a big part of who you are. It's connected to your personality and how your mind works. I talk more about this in my book, "7 Parables of the Human Identity."

Starting your talent discovery journey might seem confusing. Where do you begin? Especially if you haven't found your talent yet. I suggest looking at your parents. What are they interested in? What did they enjoy when they were kids? You don't have to do the exact same things, but because they're your parents, there might be a connection between your talents and theirs, sort of like how you might look like them. Even if you weren't raised by your biological parents, you can still get ideas from the people who took care of you. Once you've thought about that, think about the things you really like to do. For example, I really like musical instruments. I haven't learnt to play one yet, but I'm really interested in them. Maybe you're really into sports, fashion, or cooking. Whatever you're interested in is worth checking out. Even if you don't have a lot of money, you can still learn. You could go to a cooking class or try cooking new things at home.

It's never too late to try new things. Your age doesn't matter. Even if you think you're too old to do something, you can still use your talents in different ways. For example, many football players retire when they're in their 30s. They might not be able to play on a team, but they can still do other things like coaching, managing, talking about the game on TV, or being a commentator. So, don't let your age stop you from finding your talents.

Take personality and aptitude tests.

Finding your talent can be tough, especially when you're not sure what you're good at. But there are tests that can help you figure it out. These tests look at your personality and can tell you what you're strong in. By taking these tests and understanding what they say, you can learn more about yourself. This can help you use your talents in your personal life and at work.

To get started with these tests, first, choose

one that's good for you. There are many kinds, from quick online quizzes to more detailed tests given by professionals. Some popular ones include the Myers-Briggs Type Indicator, the Big Five Personality Test, and the CliftonStrengths assessment. Each one looks at different parts of your personality and can show you where you're strong.

When you take the test, be open-minded and honest. Remember, the test isn't there to judge you. It's just meant to help you understand yourself better. Read the instructions carefully, and answer the questions thoughtfully. Don't try to trick the test or get a specific result. Just be yourself and answer honestly.

After you finish the test, it's crucial to carefully look at your results and think about what they mean. Many of these tests give you detailed reports or explanations of your scores. These reports can help you understand what you're good at and where you might need improvement. Take your time to go through these reports and see how the things the test said about you relate to your life.

Pay special attention to areas where your scores are really high or really low. These could be clues about your talents and abilities.

Also, it's a good idea to talk to people you trust about your test results. Share what you learnt with your friends, family, or coworkers, and ask for their thoughts. They might see things about you that you didn't notice, and this can help you understand your talents better.

The most important part is to take action based on what you've learnt. Use the information from the test to set goals and make changes in your life. For example, if the test says you're really good at empathy, think about ways you can use that creativity in your hobbies or work.

Finally, one important thing to know is that you might have more than one talent. It took me a while to realise this. I used to think I was only good at math, but I also found out I'm good at communication and connecting with people. So, don't get confused if you discover you have more than one talent during this process. It's perfectly normal!

DEVELOPING YOUR TALENTS

In this final chapter, we'll explore how to make the most of your talents to become your best self. Looking back at my own journey, I've realised how my ability to connect with people and convey messages played a big role in shaping my purpose. But these talents needed work, like polishing a rough diamond. To truly excel, I put in a lot of effort to improve my writing and speaking skills. I understood that if I used my ability to connect wisely, I could make a positive impact on many lives. So, I learnt to express myself clearly through writing and speaking, touching the hearts of those who read or listened to my work.

But connecting and communicating were just the beginning. Over time, I also discovered my talent for critical thinking and organising ideas, like an architect planning a building. This talent helped me create a strong foundation for sharing knowledge in a way that people could easily understand and use in their lives. It not only helped me write my own books but also assist others in writing and publishing their own.

In a world full of diverse talents and potentials, the journey of personal growth and self-discovery often starts with recognising and nurturing your unique gifts. We're all born with special abilities and capacities that make us different from each other. These raw talents have the potential to become areas of great strength. While the idea of identifying and developing talents is not new, it's still crucial in today's ever-changing world.

Think about Oprah Winfrey's life. She's a famous figure known not just for her achievements, but for her amazing ability to connect with people in a very human way. Oprah's journey from a simple beginning to becoming a big name in media and culture shows the incredible power that lies in our natural talents. Even when she was young, in tough times, Oprah had a talent for talking and connecting with others. She was a great speaker and had a special gift for understanding people's feelings, even before she fully realised how talented she was.

As she went through life, Oprah discovered

that her talent for communication was her special skill. She saw that her kind nature and her gift for expressing herself could become a strength that could change lives. She understood the importance of sharing stories, talking openly about challenges, and shedding light on problems that people often ignore. Basically, Oprah turned her raw talent for connecting and communicating into a source of strength that transformed not only her life but also the lives of many others.

Oprah's story teaches us an important lesson: our natural talents are like seeds that can grow into fields of achievement, influence, and change. But this journey requires more than just recognising our talents. It needs nurturing, improvement, and a deliberate effort to turn these gifts into things we're really good at.

Our natural talents are like the first step toward becoming really good at something. Think of it like a gardener taking care of a seed, making sure it has the right conditions to grow. We need to take care of our talents too, with dedication, self-awareness, and a willingness to try new things. Our talents are like rough diamonds that need to be cut, polished, and shaped to show how amazing they really are.

In the next pages, we'll learn how to turn our raw talents into real strengths. We'll use examples from real life, along with strategies and tips, to discover the special abilities hidden inside us, waiting to become useful skills.

As we start this journey of transformation, remember that the journey itself shows how committed we are to getting better. Just like a sculptor turns a block of stone into a beautiful artwork, we can shape our raw talents into strengths that make our lives better and also help others. So, with open minds, determined hearts, and a strong desire to discover our hidden potential, let's get started on this journey to develop our raw talents into lasting strengths.

Practise. Practise Practise

In my journey of getting better at what I do, I've learnt that practice is super important. I've always been fascinated by words and how they can grab people's attention. So, I decided to get better at writing. I started with something simple - writing letters to my friends and family. These letters let me play around with different writing styles and express my thoughts and feelings in a personal way. They showed me how to tell stories that connect with people and leave a mark.

Then, as the internet grew, I tried blogging. Blogging let me share my ideas and thoughts with even more people. Each blog post was a chance to explore new topics, try out different writing styles, and get better at keeping readers interested. The feedback and conversations with my readers kept me excited about writing and encouraged me to keep improving.

During my writing journey, I also worked on a bunch of books. Not all of them got published, but they're special to me because they helped me learn. These unpublished books let me try different types of writing - like different genres and styles. They taught me a lot, both from the things that went well and the things that didn't. It's like they were my practice canvases, helping me find my own way of writing.

If you have a talent that makes you really happy, go for it with all your heart, and don't be scared. The key to getting better is practising. Remember, all the great writers, artists, musicians, and inventors started with a bit of talent, just like you.

No matter if it's writing, painting, singing, or anything else, don't hesitate to practise in different ways. Start by jotting down your thoughts in a journal, making small artworks, or singing along to your favourite songs. The more you practise, the more your talent will grow and surprise you.

Don't be worried to try new things and explore different aspects of your talent. Write short stories or poems, test out various painting methods, or experiment with different types of music. Each new thing you try will help you get better and find your own unique creative style.

Practising doesn't mean you have to be perfect; it's about getting better. Don't worry about making mistakes; you can learn from them. It's okay to try different things and discover new parts of your talent as you go. Every time you try, whether it works out or not, is a chance to learn and get better. Don't be afraid to be creative, and don't worry about what others think. Your journey is yours, and every step you take helps you grow and get stronger.

Remember, even the most famous artists and writers were once beginners. They didn't become experts overnight; it took a lot of practice and hard work. Enjoy your journey and believe that your talent will get better with time and care.

Seek guidance and mentorship

After I finished university, I stepped into a new phase of life, excited to explore the world beyond campus. But I noticed that the support I had from family and friends was not the same. I wanted someone to guide me, help me with my talents, and show me how to handle adulthood.

Surprisingly, I found mentors at my workplace. My boss and the company's owner saw something in me that I didn't see myself —a talent that needed to be developed. They shared their knowledge, experiences, and encouraged me as I learned about my job. I was working in a digital marketing agency, and this job introduced me to reading and writing. My mentors believed in the power of knowledge, and they had a library in their office. In my free time, I read books about marketing, psychology, and communication.

Then, something clicked in my mind. You don't always have to meet your mentors in person. You can learn from their words in books. During that time, every book I read became a mentor in its own way, teaching me valuable lessons and inspiring me.

Those books opened doors to a world beyond my workplace. I found mentors in the pages written by wise people who were far away from me. Authors like Seth Godin, John C Maxwell, Caroline Leaf, and Tony Robbins became my mentors through their books. They shared their knowledge and experiences, even though I couldn't meet them in person.

Reading these books gave me a treasure chest of wisdom that went beyond time and distance. The things I learnt from my mentors' writings fuelled my passion and made me want to get better at what I do. Through their words, I connected with people who had faced tough times but still succeeded. Their stories of not giving up, being creative, and finding new solutions inspired me. It was like they gave me a map to follow to reach my goals.

As I got to know more mentors, I also gained more confidence and determination. I started to see myself as part of a big group of people trying to get better and achieve success. Every mentor, whether I met them or read their books, was a chance for me to learn, grow, and become the best version of myself.

Finding mentors has been a big part of my journey. My family and friends couldn't be my mentors for my job, but I found help and support at work and in the books I read. These mentors, whether they were real people or in books, taught me a lot. They made my talents better, and they made me want to keep learning and getting better. Having mentors has really helped me grow, both in my personal life and at work. I'm excited to keep learning and discovering more with my mentors.

Take courses and workshops

Taking courses and joining workshops has been a big part of my journey to develop my talents. It's like finding mentors in books, but here, I have a teacher and a structured class. These programmes have given me great guidance, hands-on experience, and a supportive place to learn. They've really helped me get better at what I do.

One programme that really helped me was a public speaking workshop. I knew that being a good speaker would be important for my work and my personal life. Even though it cost money, I thought it was worth it. The workshop gave me tools, tricks, and the confidence to be a better speaker.

The teacher, who was a very experienced speaker, was like a mentor. They shared their wisdom and what they learnt over many years. In the class, I felt like I was on a team with others who also wanted to get better at public speaking. We all helped and supported each other in our learning journey.

During the workshop, I got to do many exercises and practise what I was learning. The instructor and my classmates gave me helpful feedback. This helped me see where I needed to improve and also celebrate how much I was getting better.

Taking workshops and courses has been really good for me. It goes hand in hand with what I learn from books. Books give me lots of knowledge and ideas, but workshops and courses are more like hands-on training. They help me develop my skills. Using both methods together has been great for making my talents better and helping me grow as a person.

It's super important to sign up for workshops, even if they cost money. They give you a focused and organised way to learn. You can make big progress in a short time. Having an expert instructor is so valuable. They can give you personal feedback and teach you what you need for your goals.

Plus, these workshops let you meet others who are interested in the same things. You can work together, make friends, and share ideas. It makes learning even more fun and opens up new possibilities for success.

As we near the end of this book, I want to share some last thoughts to keep you inspired on your journey of self-discovery and personal growth. Finding your unique path in life isn't always easy, but it's a journey that can profoundly change your life for the better.

Throughout these pages, we've explored various ideas, methods, and tips to help you unlock your inner potential. I hope the information in this book has given you a useful set of tools – like a toolkit – that can help you navigate toward a life that's both fulfilling and meaningful.

Figuring out your own path, your true purpose, can be hard. It might require looking inside yourself, trying new things, and stepping outside your comfort zone. But it's through this journey that you can discover what truly excites you, what you're good at, and what makes you special.

Don't forget, it's not about comparing yourself to others or trying to live up to someone else's idea of success. Your journey is about embracing who you are and recognising the path that feels right for you, deep inside.

As you move forward, I encourage you to carry the lessons you've learnt from this book with you. Use them as a guide, like a compass, to help you through life's challenges. And as you follow your unique path, may you discover fulfilment, purpose, and a life full of meaning and authenticity.

REFLECTION

1. Do you believe in talents? Have you discovered yours yet?

2. Have you received any feedback or compliments from others regarding your skills or abilities? What do people often turn to you for help or advice with?

3. What are the activities or tasks that you find most enjoyable and effortless? When do you feel "in the zone" and lose track of time?

4. Reflect on your past experiences and the roles you've held. What aspects of these experiences brought you the most satisfaction and a sense of accomplishment?

5. Consider your role models or people you admire. What talents or qualities in them resonate with you?

A MESSAGE FROM KELVIN

First and foremost, I want to express my heartfelt gratitude for taking the time to read this book. Your engagement means the world to me.

I'm Kelvin, the author, and I'm excited to share something special with you. If you've found my book inspiring and believe it could make a positive impact on a larger scale, I invite you to consider sharing it with event organisers you may know.

My mission is straightforward: to inspire and empower individuals to reach their full potential. My talks are interactive, relatable, and filled with real-life examples. They aim to leave audiences with practical insights and a renewed sense of purpose.

By sharing my book with event organisers, you can help create an opportunity for others to experience this empowerment. Whether it's at a conference, school, or any gathering, my goal is to spark positive transformations wherever I go.

Your simple act of passing on my book could lead to an enriching and memorable experience for a wider audience. I believe that together, we can inspire greatness in even more individuals.

If you know an event organiser who might resonate with my message and style, please don't hesitate to share my book and contact information with them:

Email: kelvin@kayveebooks.com

Your support and initiative can amplify the impact of our message of inspiration. Let's empower others to reach their full potential!

ABOUT THE AUTHOR

Kelvin Osondu is a highly motivated individual with a passion for writing and helping others. At just 16 years old, he wrote his first book, setting the foundation for a career that combines his love of writing and desire to make a positive impact on the world.

He is an author with several self-help books under his belt. During the day, he helps businesses grow online using marketing strategies. He is also a public speaker and trainer.

With his many talents and unwavering dedication to his craft, Kelvin Osondu is a true inspiration to all those around him.

More Books By Kelvin

The Intentional Student

7 Parables of the Human Identity

Emotions 101

Printed in Great Britain
by Amazon